Shopping

A ZEBRA BOOK

Written by Sue Tarsky
Illustrated by David Bennett

PUBLISHED BY
WALKER BOOKS
LONDON

There are lots of things in shops.

toys

clothes

What can you see?

There are all kinds of shoes.

sandal

slipper

lace-up shoe

boot

What kind do you wear?

Trying on shoes.

Which colour do you like best?

These are not for you!

runner's

frogman's

spaceman's

clown's

Do you know who wears them?

Jumpers are in the clothes shop.

too small

too big

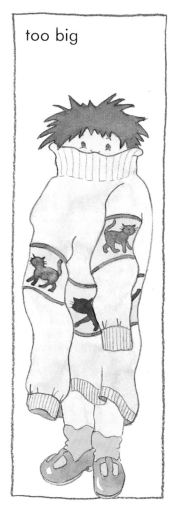

Some jumpers fit just right.

polo neck jumper

jumper with
a hood

What kinds of jumpers do you have?

Fruit is in the fruit shop.

soft grapes

hard apples

round oranges

long bananas

What other fruits do you eat?

You can go to the grocery shop.

box

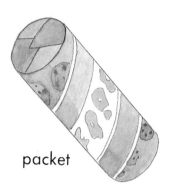

packet

jar

tin

How do you open these?

The music shop is full of noise.

What sounds do these instruments make?

Books are in the book shop.

Some books have words.

THE 3 BEARS

That's upside down!

Some books don't have words.

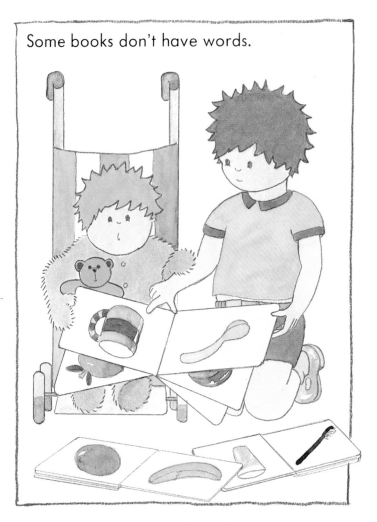

What is your favourite book?

Animals are in the pet shop.

goldfish

puppies   kittens

How many animals can you count?

There are presents to buy in shops.

something for dad

something for mum

Who else do you buy presents for?

The sports shop is fun.

balls

tennis racket

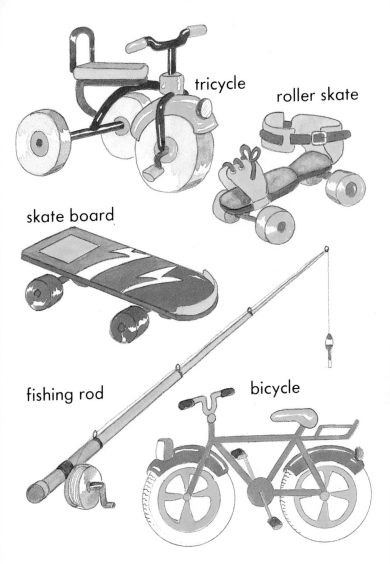

tricycle

roller skate

skate board

fishing rod

bicycle

How do you use these?

The toy shop has toys.

a toy you push

a toy you pull

a toy you cuddle

a toy you ride

What toy would you choose?

You carry your parcels home.

a light
parcel

a heavy
parcel

You can read your new book.

What will you buy next time?